For Clint—my "guy in the chair." — A.H.E.

For Amos, Owen, and Margo. — L.G.

This biography of Steve Ditko was created without the involvement or endorsement of Mr. Ditko or the companies with which he has been associated.

Text copyright © 2023 Annie Hunter Eriksen
Illustrations copyright © 2023 Lee Gatlin

First published in 2023 by Page Street Kids
an imprint of
Page Street Publishing Co.
27 Congress Street, Suite 1511
Salem, MA 01970
www.pagestreetpublishing.com

Distributed by Macmillan, sales in Canada by The Canadian Manda Group

23 24 25 26 27 CCO 5 4 3 2 1
ISBN-13: 978-1-64567-710-9
ISBN-10: 1-64567-710-9

CIP data for this book is available from the Library of Congress.

This book was typeset in Lovely Crafter. The illustrations were done using mixed media.
Cover and book design by Melia Parsloe for Page Street Kids
Edited by Kayla Tostevin for Page Street Kids

Printed and bound in Shenzhen, Guangdong, China

Page Street Publishing uses only materials from suppliers who are committed to responsible and sustainable forest management.

Page Street Publishing protects our planet by donating to nonprofits like The Trustees, which focuses on local land conservation.

ALONG CAME A RADIOACTIVE SPIDER

Strange Steve Ditko and the Creation of Spider-Man
An Unauthorized Biography

ANNIE HUNTER ERIKSEN   ILLUSTRATED BY LEE GATLIN

PAGE STREET KIDS

There was absolutely nothing strange about comic book artist Steve Ditko. His life was an open book.

He was a real people person—especially toward his fans.

And his artwork? Totally by-the-book.

Okay . . . so Steve Ditko wasn't really like the rest of the artists at Marvel Comics, but the same could be said about his—yes, Steve's!—most famous creation:

SPIDER-MAN.

There was definitely something strange about Spider-Man.

He was thin and agile like an acrobat, not mighty and muscular. His powers of clinging to walls and spinning webs were more creepy-crawly than conventional.

And with the mask off, Peter Parker wasn't charming and cool like quarterback Flash Thompson at Midtown High.

He stumbled over his words as much as he stumbled over his piles of books.

Where did a strange wall-crawling hero and his even stranger web of stories begin?

Spidey's origin story started like a radioactive spider bite: in the palm of Steve's hand.

Long before Spider-Man, there was just Steve, a kid who loved comics. Back then, the Great Depression made putting food on the table tough, especially for families as big (and ravenous) as Steve's.

Luckily, newspapers were cheap—and they had comics. Steve and his father devoured the weekly strips while his mother helped save each one, sewing a whole year's worth into one big homemade book.

It wasn't strange that Steve grew up to become a professional comic book artist. Steve was strange because of his style.

Between Steve's pages were loners whose eyeballs—not muscles— bulged. Monsters shrouded in shadows, not heroes costumed in capes. Otherworldly beings draped in dense fog, not pretty damsels in distress.

Marvel editor Stan Lee loved *strange*—it's why Steve landed his job as an artist. The two couldn't have been any more different from each other.

Stan was boisterous like a constant parade. Steve was studious and just trying to get his work done. Stan acted out story plots while playing the ocarina. Steve was seriously just trying to get his work done.

But the dynamic duo had a marvelous method:

FOOSH

Stan tossed a spellbinding
story to Steve.

Steve mapped out the comic, following his instincts like a compass. He sprinkled in shifting perspectives, made a mastery of emotions, and drew distorted forms.

Still, Steve wasn't the artist behind the bestsellers like *Captain America* or *The Fantastic Four.* That honor went to Jack "The King" Kirby, whose handsome heroes threw powerful punches on every page. It seemed as if no artist could take the crown from The King.

It wasn't strange when Stan and The King teamed up yet again for their new story: a boy, a magic ring, and a transformation into the grown-up superhero named "Spiderman."

SHOOM

Steve's job was to illustrate the new comic, but when it landed on his desk, something felt off. Spiderman was just another repetitive brave and brawny hero! Steve itched to break the mold in the best way he knew how—by making Spiderman strange.

All the other artists stayed inside the lines of their writers' stories.

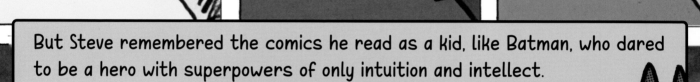

But Steve remembered the comics he read as a kid, like Batman, who dared to be a hero with superpowers of only intuition and intellect.

And The Spirit, a genre-defying comic strip with fresh chapters that drew him across town every Sunday with his little brother Pat in tow—even in a blizzard so fierce he had to carry Pat as their boots filled with snow.

Those were the kinds of stories Steve wanted to tell: stories so spellbinding, readers would want to sew them into one big homemade book. Ones worth braving storms for. Steve did what he did best: he got to work.

SQUEEP
SQUEEP

He erased the magic ring and said goodbye to The King's grown-up hero.

WA-WHOP!

Hello, Peter Parker! Just a normal, perpetually awkward teen, when along came a radioactive spider and . . .

TWNNNNG!

...a bite to spin a new
kind of origin story.

The higher-ups at Marvel hemmed and hawed, but to Steve, this new (hyphenated!) Spider-Man made sense. *Spidey* sense.

Spider-Man became famous overnight and was soon greenlit to star in his own series. Suddenly, Steve found himself writing and drawing *Spider-Man*—a comic book history first.

POW!

He had dethroned The King.

Steve's Spider-Man didn't just fight. He danced with his enemies. And Steve's villains weren't run-of-the-mill bad guys.

But Steve introduced Spidey's greatest challenge: himself. The moments when Spidey relied on inner strength—not super-strength—were the ones that made Steve comic book royalty.

Now everyone wanted a piece of Steve.

But just like Peter Parker, Steve was a fish out of water when it came to being mainstream. The noise from being centerstage was too loud—even if it was praise for his web-slinging creation!

He evaded questions like Spidey dodging the Green Goblin's pumpkin bombs.

He stuck to walls when barraged by fans.

Perhaps it was strange that Steve swung away from the spotlight and into the quiet where he could focus on creating new stories. But if escaping the pressure of being a celebrity was strange, then he didn't want to be ordinary.

VOOOOSH
and spiraling cosmos twisting with psychedelic spells into a story universes away,
SPAAANG
and at its center was a doctor who found selflessness by becoming the defender of Earth, the Master of the Mystic Arts.
The comic was out of this world . . . and his most fitting work yet! Steve named him
DOCTOR STRANGE.

IF THIS BE MY DESTINY . . . !

Steve Ditko was born on November 2nd, 1927, in Johnstown, Pennsylvania. Despite the crushing backdrop of the Great Depression, Steve had a wealth of love and support from his family. His father, Stephen, was a first-generation American who passed on to Steve a love of drawing and comics. Steve's mother, Anna, made Steve and his best friend authentic costumes from his favorite comic, *Batman*.

After serving in the army, Steve returned to the States to fulfill his destiny in becoming a comic book artist. *The* Jerry Robinson of *Batman* was teaching at The Cartoonists & Illustrators School in New York City, and Steve was determined to learn from the best. Here, Steve's style would flourish into something utterly unique.

SPIDEY SHRUGGED

In 1962, *Amazing Fantasy* #15 introduced Spider-Man. While there are conflicting accounts as to how Spidey was created, the one Steve remembered involved recognizing that Spiderman was a recycled version of a Joe Simon hero called The Fly.

Steve drew—and plotted—*Spider-Man* for 38 issues. *The Amazing Spider-Man* issue #33 is considered to be his crowning achievement. Trapped beneath a mountain of machinery and up against a ticking countdown to save his aunt, Spider-Man reaches beyond his limits and heaves himself free in five nail-biting pages. Steve's escalating tension in his art and storytelling make this one of the greatest comics of all time.

Not surprisingly, there are contradicting stories as to why Steve abruptly left Marvel. Could it have been a clash between Stan Lee's uncanny knack for commercial success and Steve's sole intent on creating art for art's sake? Or was it a fight over the origin story of the Green Goblin? Regardless, in 1966 Steve left Marvel and Spider-Man, never to return again.

STEVE DITKO WOULD HATE THIS BOOK

Steve wouldn't dip his toes in mainstream success again—not that he much cared. To understand Steve's post-Marvel characters like The Question and Mr. A—and Steve himself—is to understand the philosophy of Objectivism. Black is black. White is white. And there is nothing in between.

There are only a handful of published photographs of Steve. He had refused interviews since 1968 and declared author Blake Bell's biography on him a "poison sandwich." He also possessed an unwavering work ethic, an uncompromising moral code, and a devout dedication to his family. The prodigal son would return to Johnstown twice a year, and for Christmas, Steve presented his family with holiday comics he had made, just like those from his childhood.

As the 2007 *BBC* documentary *In Search of Steve Ditko* discovered (in which Steve did not make an appearance), the distinct honor of meeting Steve Ditko meant

following one rule: you *don't* talk about Ditko. Sure, you'd leave with a handful of original Ditko comics, but also with the personal responsibility of keeping such an experience to yourself. There was nothing in between.

BIBLIOGRAPHY

Bell, Blake. *Strange and Stranger: The World of Steve Ditko*. Fantagraphics Books, 2008.

Boyd Maclean, Peter, and Jonathan Ross. "In Search of Steve Ditko (2007) - YouTube." *YouTube*, BBC, 16 Sept. 2007, https://www.youtube.com/watch?v=3gwDnhMO8is.

Cronin, Brian. "Comic Legends: Was Steve Ditko Really a Recluse?" CBR, 13 July 2018, https://www.cbr.com/steve-ditko-recluse-truth/

Dean, Michael. "Steve Ditko 1927-2018." *The Comics Journal*, 6 July 2018, https://www.tcj.com/steve-ditko-1927-2018/

Ditko, Steve, and Stan Lee. *Ditko Is . . . Amazing!* Marvel, 2019.

Riesman, Abraham. "The Creator of Doctor Strange Will Not See You Now." *Vulture*, 15 Nov. 2016, https://www.vulture.com/2016/11/steve-ditko-doctor-strange-c-v-r.html